# ABUNDANCE OF ONE

DABO DAVIES

THE ABUNDANCE OF ONE by Dabo Davies

Published by D.H Davies Global

DH DAVIES GLOBAL LONDON

UNITED KINGDOM

WWW.DHDAVIES.ORG

This book or portion thereof may not be reproduced in any form, stored in a retrieval system or transmitted in any form by any means- electronic, mechanical, photocopy, recording, or otherwise- without the prior written permission of the publisher.

PRINTED IN UNITED KINGDOM **ISBN:** 9798645969462

Copyright 2020, by Dabo Davies

All rights reserved.

## *Appreciation*

All that I know is a total of what I have been taught, first, by the Holy Spirit, and from all those who have taught me in my journey, both directly and indirectly.

I am forever grateful to the countless exceptional people who, by their commitment and devotion to becoming the best they could be, have inspired me to do the same.

I am ever mindful of the unmatched love, prayer, support, and patience of my precious wife, Elizabeth.

To my countless partners worldwide who through their love and passion have shown kindness and support,
I say THANK YOU!

## *Dedication*

To my lovely children in whom I believe there is at least one gift that will bring them to a place of significance.

To the billions of individuals destined to discover, develop, and deploy that one gift, skill, or talent that has the potential to change their life and everyone that will encounter them

To all the leaders who I have met along the way, whose willingness to cultivate their one gift allowed me to find mine and brought me to a place of maturity.

*ABUNDANCE OF ONE*

# Table of Contents

APPRECIATION ......................................................................... v
DEDICATION .......................................................................... vii
TABLE OF CONTENTS ............................................................ ix
INTRODUCTION ....................................................................... 1
**CHAPTER ONE**: What's In Your Hand? ............................... 7
   Understanding Conceptualization ...................................... 10
   Two Lessons Learned From How To Become Jesus' Disciple .... 16
   Have You Identified '*Your Blessings?*' ............................... 18
   Dependencies ....................................................................... 23
   What Are You Waiting For? ................................................. 26
   Our Hands Have Been Blessed To Dress And Keep Our Garden ... 29
   Amazon: One Man, One Idea ............................................... 34
   Focus On Yourself - Avoid Comparison ............................. 37
**CHAPTER TWO**: Start Before You Are Ready! ................. 41
   Start In The Midst Of Uncertainties/ Overcome The Fear Of The Unknown ............................................................. 43
   Time Is Valuable .................................................................. 43
   Start With the Right Attitude ............................................... 44

**CHAPTER THREE:** Set Yourself Up For Success ............................. 51
   First, Excitement Is Not Enough! ..................................... 53
   Why Not Sit Down, Count, And Think Before You Start? ......... 55
   Think and Pray .............................................................. 59
   Lessons From King David .................................................. 61
   God Can Help You Arrive At The Answers You Seek ............... 63
   Reach Out For Insight ..................................................... 64

**CHAPTER FOUR:** When One Feels Like None ............................... 67
   Lincoln's One .................................................................. 69
   Something out of Nothing ................................................. 70
   What's Your *One*? ........................................................... 71
   The Man Who Buried Abundance ....................................... 72
   You'll Account For One ..................................................... 75

**CHAPTER FIVE:** The Multiplier Effect ........................................ 77
   McDonald's Franchise ....................................................... 79
   Faith Franchise ............................................................... 80

**CHAPTER SIX:** Nurturing Your Dream ....................................... 85
   Mlk: The Man Who Had Been To The Future: ...................... 87
   You Have A Dream Even If You Aren't Mlk .......................... 89

**CHAPTER SEVEN:** How To Bite And Breathe! .............................. 101
   Derek Redmond .............................................................. 102
   Thomas Edison ............................................................... 105
   Face Your Fears .............................................................. 106
   Now, How Do You Face Your Fear? .................................... 107
   Choosing Faith Over Fear .................................................. 109
   The Wisdom of Patience ................................................... 110

**CHAPTER EIGHT:** Leveraging Divine Advantage .......................... 115
   Intimacy And Foresight .................................................... 118
   Bouncing Back After Suffering Great Loss .......................... 120
   David's Inquiry ............................................................... 122

## Introduction

We cannot separate the desire for accomplishments and crave for progress from human experience. The light of hope is the force that keeps us alive. The reason why you get up in the morning and keep going till late in the night is, deep down, you probably believe you deserve more and can achieve more. But why not?

How many times have you found yourself stuck somewhere in the middle of desire and contentment, optimism and dread, faith, and doubts? You begin to contemplate the possibilities of the future as estimated by the provisions of today. So, you ask, is there any freedom from the limits of my past? Do I have anything to exchange for a better life?

You see, starting something can often seem overwhelming and complicated whether it is starting a business, a new career, a new job, or even a relationship. Yet, how can you arrive until you have set off for your journey?

Indeed, there are so many things you often consider that range from the known to the unknown. Yet, have you ever taken some time to question your ostensible perspective about who you are, what you have, and the things you can achieve?

I want you to understand that those things that seem to stand between you, the promises and dreams in your life might not be so unmovable. You need to think again when next you are tempted to wait till you've got it all figured out before you set out for something significant. Or how long will you continue to walk past that ONE-thing and miss the realities of your inner abundance? It's time you know the power of ONE!

## Transcending the realm of the unknown

For the majority of people, it is the invisible challenge that lies between the known and the unknown that develops into fear and eventually stops them from the initiation stage of notable accomplishments. So, an individual can conceive something, but the challenge of where they are and where they are going eventually cripples them till, they are unable to move.

So, it's like when God tells you that, He would expand your influence to several nations, and there you are in one little place, one village, one community, with few loved ones, trying to navigate your way from that point to greatness.

Unfortunately, a lot of times, if you are not careful, you'll find that it is just that line between the known and the unknown that cripples you and sabotages your effort.

## You need to X-ray your mentality

Why is it hard to realize that the difference between the place of promise and the seasons of manifestation of the purpose of God for your life is your mindset? Indeed, your life will always revolve around your most dominant thought. No wonder, King Solomon said, *"For as he thinketh in his heart, so is he..."* **(Proverbs 23:7)**.

My question for you is, to what extent can you comprehend greatness in your mind? Are you ready to get uncomfortable with mediocrity? Do you know the power of setting out for greatness even if it means starting with ONE thing before the other? Do you want to know how to navigate from nothing to plenty?

If your answer to any of these questions is yes, then you can expect to experience a mind shift as you read this book. I want you to know that you can move from a life of lack to a new life in Abundance in every way.

Furthermore, you will realize that God is not partial in His dealings with anyone. Anything good you see God do for somebody can be replicated in your life. Indeed, you can become great! All you need is to learn how to nurture the seed of greatness that God has reserved in you. So, I can comfortably say, you have in your possession the book that will help you accomplish this. Again, you have that ONE seed that will change your world.

Why don't you take another step forward with your life by embracing a new reality? Do you know that you have been custom-built to make a difference in life? Now, talking about discovering your hidden treasures, surely, you don't need to look too far beyond this precious jewel in your hand right now. I'm certain that, you are holding the torch with which you can lit up your inner treasure house. So, get ready for some new discoveries.

Besides, I love this quote from the popular Television Show Host, Oprah Winfrey which says "if you look at what you have in your life you will always have more, but if you look at what you don't have in your life, you will never have enough"

So, don't wait till you have plenty before you begin a journey into abundance, start from where you are. Start from reading this book carefully and diligently. Focus on yourself and no other person for that change that you desire. God is interested in your progress.

At this juncture, I'll like to ask, what has God committed into your hand? Which specific area in life has God placed your innate influence? What singular assignment has God given to you? I believe strongly that by the inspiration of the Holy Spirit, you will learn how to stay focused on that one thing that God has committed into our hands and watch the greatness that emerges from it.

Furthermore, we shall examine the place of evaluation as we reach for desired goals. For instance, if you need to take a flight from the United Kingdom to the Bahamas, after establishing your destination, next is to make an inquiry about the cost of the flight, if not your trip will remain a mere contemplation in your mind.

You will learn the importance of spending quality time thinking through what it will cost you to move from where you are to where you want to be. This book promises to let you in on scriptural principles and applicable wisdom for strategic thinking which always produces excellent results. Yes! Prayer is the key, and strategic thinking will apply this key to any door until it opens for you. However, how can a mind think through the maze of impossibility and mindset of insufficiency, a mind that always crashes ONE to zero? It is time to stop crucifying our heroes! Like the words of Caiaphas, the High Priest, *"...consider that it is expedient for us, that ONE man should die for the people, and that the whole nation perish not."* **(John 11:50).** That ONE MAN was Jesus!

How long will you continue to lose faith in little beginnings? Don't you think it's time to rediscover the precious things that have been placed in you, craving for nurture and manifestation? It is time to discern your times and seasons, so you can walk at the pace of divine progress.

I believe very strongly that you will have an encounter with the Holy Spirit from the pages of this book that will inspire your mind and heart till you are able to take the right steps that will lead you into your desired abundance.

*God Bless You!*

# CHAPTER One

## What's In Your Hand?

> *Then the Lord said to him, "What is that in your hand?" "A staff," he replied.*
> **- Exodus 4:2**

Starting something new can often seem overwhelming and complicated. Whether you are starting a business, a political career, a new job, or even a relationship.

The truth is, there are so many things you must consider, from the known to the unknown. For most people, the invisible challenge that lies between the known and the unknown is their obstacle. This challenge often produces fear, stopping them dead in their tracks and unable to reach the initiation stage.

As a result, this crippling fear has resulted in houses full of seeds that were never planted. These seeds had the potential of becoming great oak trees but never got the chance to explore this ability. Seeds that could have grown taller than buildings now sit on the shelf in a tin can in a building, for they never got the opportunity to live up to their potential.

The fact is, starting anything, as simple as it appears is a process that requires a great deal of thought and careful analysis. And, it is important at this point not to mistake conceiving an idea from the initiation phase: the act of actually bringing your idea to a point where work is demanded.

Conception (conceiving an idea), which is the mental phase precedes the initiation phase. Here, the idea first comes into your mind in the form of inspiration. For instance, before there were electric cars, someone conceived the idea. So, it went from existing solely in the mind to a point where it becomes capable of being touched, tested, and then driven. At this point, it is no longer vague, imaginary, or elusive, but now has actual physical existence. It becomes physically perceptible.

There are individuals who at this present time have conceived various ideas, such as a form of technology that can transform how we communicate, Infrastructure that can transform how we travel, food, and nutrition that can ease the burden on medical science and transform how we live. But the problem is, these ideas are still in the conception stage, and perhaps have been there for ages, and may never materialise.

On the other hand, initiation is quite different. It's simply the act of beginning a thing.

In Project Management, The Project Initiation Phase is the first phase in the Project Management Life-Cycle. And it involves starting up a new project. This consists of defining the objectives, scope, purpose, and deliverables (tangible or intangible goods or services produced as a result of a project that is intended to be delivered to a client) to be produced. Also, the initiation phase involves setting up a project team, a project office, and so on. All these at this stage are no longer mental exercises or calibration but the actual work.

## ♟ UNDERSTANDING CONCEPTUALIZATION

Let's consider an incident in the bible that would provide more insight into this concept. In the book of Luke, Jesus was educating those aspiring to be His disciples on the cost of discipleship. It is amazing to see how explicit He was. He gave an example of what a conception stage looks like. This can be found in Luke chapter 4:25-33:

> **Luke 14:25-33 The Living Bible (TLB)**
>
> ²⁵ Great crowds were following him. He turned around and addressed them as follows:
>
> ²⁶ "Anyone who wants to be my follower must love me far more than he does his own father, mother, wife, children, brothers, or sisters—yes, more than his own life—otherwise he cannot be my disciple.
>
> ²⁷ And no one can be my disciple who does not carry his own cross and follow me.
>
> ²⁸ "But don't begin until you count the cost. For who would begin construction of a building without first getting estimates and then checking to see if he has enough money to pay the bills?

> ²⁹ Otherwise, he might complete only the foundation before running out of funds. And then how everyone would laugh!
>
> ³⁰ "'See that fellow there?' they would mock. 'He started that building and ran out of money before it was finished!'
>
> ³¹ "Or what king would ever dream of going to war without first sitting down with his counsellors and discussing whether his army of 10,000 is strong enough to defeat the 20,000 men who are marching against him?
>
> ³² "If the decision is negative, then while the enemy troops are still far away, he will send a truce team to discuss terms of peace.
>
> ³³ So no one can become my disciple unless he first sits down and counts his blessings—and then renounces them all for me.

Taking the event in the above bible verse into context, it highlights the importance of conceptualization, a careful analysis that must be considered whether we are building with many or just a few. At this stage, our mind begins to process certain questions like, do we start the project or not? Do we start in the first quarter or not? What is the specific number of human resources required in the project team? What particular skills do we require in the project team? How much space do we need for an office? What systems, technology, or methodology should be applied, etc?

Let us take a closer look at some key points I gleaned from the above passage:

1. **Count** – This means to check over the separate units or groups of a collection one by one to determine the total number

   - Also, it means to calculate or compute.
   - Considering the word calculate; this means determining something by reasoning, common sense, or practical experience.

Thus, from these definitions, we can infer that to count can be summarised as a way to determine by reasoning, common sense, or practical experience.

2. **Cost** – This is the price paid to acquire, produce, accomplish, or maintain anything.

In the bible passage we just read, Jesus was highlighting the importance of planning, organizing, and strategizing.

Identifying the importance of preparation before the performance. Surprisingly, this is an area that can be easily neglected, especially in this day and age.

> *"There are risks and costs to a program of action. But they are far less than the long-range risks and costs of comfortable inaction"*
>
> **- John F. Kennedy**
> (35th President of the United States)

It appears that many do not seem to effectively apply their reasoning and practical experience in counting the cost. They tend to be reluctant in considering the bill, the investment required, the necessary sacrifices and commitment needed to produce, accomplish, or maintain what they desire.

The concept or idea of having something is very pleasing without properly evaluating the corresponding commitment attached to it.

The truth is, the idea of owning something can bring great pleasure when you haven't counted the cost. And I believe that this is one of the reasons for many abandoned projects, abandoned visions, and even abandoned relationships. Don't you agree?

Take a look at the picture of a family on holiday, basking in the sun, or playing on the beach often fascinates the mind. But the commitment and dedication required to bring that family to that point where they are all happy, or where that luxurious holiday is affordable can be easily ignored.

Also, it is at the point of counting the cost that many become overwhelmed by the work and task of accomplishing such a great idea.

The question then is, how do we effectively balance the thinking and acting stage without any injustice to one?

The fact is, almost everyone can think, conceive an idea, but the act of actually doing or bringing that idea to life requires a huge amount of discipline and commitment. Taking action involves some measure of risk, but that is life and there is a risk element in almost everything we do, no matter how small and immeasurable it is.

It can, therefore, be said that only those who are courageous, fearless, and focused enough can get past the conception stage.

Likewise, it is important to know that *conceptualizing* an idea is totally different from *crystallizing* it. This is because conceptualizing can happen within split seconds while crystallizing requires some level of work. Indeed, it involves various processes and practical steps.

To crystallize is to give definite or concrete form to something. It can also point us to the word **structure** – something built or constructed. The building of something, whether an object, business or even a relationship involves joining things together, which gradually comes into form.

In finance, the word crystallize means 'to *convert or be converted from a floating charge into a fixed charge.*' To make an idea secure, immovable, or established requires some amount of work and commitment.

Furthermore, in verse 33 of the passage, we read the powerful words of Jesus.

> "So, no one can become my disciple unless he first sits down and counts his blessings—and then renounces them all for me."

## TWO LESSONS LEARNED FROM HOW TO BECOME JESUS' DISCIPLE

1. Sit down
2. Count your blessing

The first point was to *sit down*, which indicates a position where you inquire into or deliberate over a matter. In this position, you can ask questions that will help you to analyse and reason logically. Also, you can think carefully about the matter at hand, especially before making a very important decision. Asking the necessary questions allows you to explore, investigate, scrutinize, and examine your options carefully before making any serious commitments.

What is the outcome of all this? Actions that come after a sit-down position is premeditated, deliberate, planned, and intentional rather than left to chance. It implies giving the matter at hand all of your attention.

The next point he made was to *count your blessing.*

Your blessing in this context is what you already have. What you have been given. What you have at your disposal and in your control. And this point requires you to first identify what you have, knowing what is available to you and properly evaluating them. Because if you must count the blessing, that blessing must be tangible. Counting involves numbering, calculating, or computing, and you can only number what is available.

Consider that He did not tell them to count what they are expecting, but to count their blessings. Therefore, ask yourself, what resources are available to me with regard to the commitment I am about to make?

What human resources do I have to effectively accomplish this task?

How many people do I require in my team to fully impact the community?

Does what I have in my bank account line up with the demands of the business?

Do I have the academic qualification to join this organization?

Do I need more time to gather resources before launching this idea?

Do I need to under-study someone or another organization before announcing my new move?

So, what's your next move? Have you counted your blessings?

This is interesting because Jesus will not make mention of *'your blessing'* if He does not think or know that you have one. The fact is, everyone has something. But the problem is, it's either we have failed to identify it, refused to develop it, do not know how to maximize it, or we spend too much time been distracted by looking at other peoples' blessings. Our inability to identify what we have is born out of our constant undermining and devaluing of what we possess. The more you lust after and place emphasis on another person's gifts and talents, the less you appreciate and engage yours.

## HAVE YOU IDENTIFIED '*YOUR BLESSINGS*?'

According to the bible passage we read, Jesus took the time to highlight how important it is for His disciples to sit-down and identify their available blessing before embarking on the journey of being His partners, His co-laborers, His associates and followers.

Before you join that organization, start that business, join that political party, embark on that bag-packing journey, relocate to that seemingly fruitful country or city, have you taken the time to sit down and count your blessings?

Have you checked your resources against the demands of that new location, or are you only excited about the prospect of relocating? Have you taken the time to consider the associated cost of running the business on a daily basis for a year, or are you just excited about the prospect of a good profit?

Do you know that it is always a different issue managing another person's business temporarily than owning and running one yourself? Have you thought of what will be required of you when the buck stops with you? When all decisions are approved by you? When everyone depends on your direction? When the success or failure of the organisation rests on your leadership skills?

Have you thought of the fact that being a member of a political party is different from running for public office? Have you counted the cost? Have you counted your blessings? Have you checked your available resources, either human or financial? Have you juxtaposed all this against the opposition?

Perhaps you are just excited about the prospects of occupying a politically elected office? But at what cost?

Let us paint a scenario; imagine you have a family of four, and presently live in a 3-bedroom flat. Given that, because of the size of your family, you have a desire to live in a 5-bedroom house of your own and have taken the first step to search for properties in your desired location.

Excitingly, you find a property, which is strategically located near very good schools for your children, close to the local grocery stores, public transportation, and local playgrounds. All these things wrapped up in one opportunity looks superb and is too good to miss. Consequently, you get overly excited and decided to move in immediately.

You check the cost, and it is on sale for £500,000, with a 10% deposit requested to process a mortgage application. This means you are technically in need of £50,000. After all the excitement, you are brought to the reality of practical steps in living in that house, which of course has conditions attached to it.

**These conditions are**

1. Provide 10% of £500,000 (which is £50,000)
2. Have a good credit score
3. Have a household income of over £80,000 annually

4. Show proof of funds in your bank account
5. Show proof of employment
6. Show proof of the right to live in the country of your residence

With the above list, it is very easy to sit down and count your blessings. For instance, if you can produce the 10% but do not have a good credit score, your next thoughts will be, how do I get my credit score up? How long does it take to get this score up? What do I need to do to correct this? As a matter of fact, following this process will open you to understanding the power of credit, the importance of keeping your credit positive always.

If this family can sit down and count their blessing, they may not move into that house immediately, but they can set up a 6-months to 1-year plan, get their credit sorted, and move into that property. They may suffer the pain of a temporary setback, but for the lasting benefit of a future fulfilment – a 5-bedroom house.

On the other hand, there are many people who will run away from the discipline of analysing the process in relation to what they have. They would rather stay where they are in that 3-

bedroom flat rather than to sit-down, count their blessings, and perhaps get that property in the next six months to one year.

This was what Jesus was talking about; Do not get carried away with the excitement and prospect of becoming a follower, or in this case, living in a property of your dreams without having to sit down and count your blessing, critically analysing what resources you have, or can lay hold of.

I've realized that a large number of people would rather not put in the work needed to count the cost. And more often than not, they give unreasonable excuses for their unwillingness to critically analyse and skilfully plan.

Are you willing to commit your strength and intellect to the task of evaluating your options before embarking on a project? Or are you with those who give excuses?

Another matter to consider is the fact that God has put in us every potential that is required for us to become better. A juniper tree has the potential to become a forest: its potential is its seed. And all creation has received the capacity to be fruitful and multiply. I believe this includes ideas, innovations, business strategies, and much more.

While people may not always literally multiply themselves, what they have within or bring to the table can multiply, like their ideas, skills, creativity, resources, etc. This is an innate potential God puts in everything.

Having the potential to multiply simply denotes that there are dependencies.

## ♟ DEPENDENCIES

There's a popular saying that no man is an island. This is a great truth. We are all dependent on each other and society as a whole to serve our needs, and generate momentum as a race.

The same scenario and logic are reflected in the domain of project management. No activity or task exists in isolation. Each item relies on the output of another activity in some way and contributes to the end result of the project.

Consequently, the relationship between the two tasks is defined as the dependency between them. In the world around you, a dependency is the state of existence of a being or an item such that its stability is dictated by another being or resource.

*For example*, children are dependent on their parents for care and sustenance. Likewise, the elderly is often dependent on their children for the same. And workers are mostly dependent on establishments for money and income.

In the setting of a project, the definition of dependency shifts to a certain degree.

A project dependency is a logical, constraint-based, or preferential relationship between two activities or tasks such that the initiation or completion of one is reliant on the completion or initiation of the other.

*For example,* if you are painting a canvas, the application of oil paint is one activity, and preparing the canvas is another.

You cannot use the paint unless the surface has been brushed with the primer.

This means, one activity is dependent on the other.

If the primer is not available for 3 days because there's a shortage in supply, the painting completion will be delayed by 3 days because you won't be able to start your work.

This is what we see with regards to what God has embedded on our inside, or if I would say given to us as either a gift or a promise. If they are not CULTIVATED, they will be there but remain dormant despite the fact that they have the potential to multiply but may never come to that point.

For some of us, what God has given us in the form of an idea, skill, or even spiritual gifts can remain dormant for our entire life if we don't get to work on them.

Let me paint another scenario to illustrate this point. Imagine you are the mother or father to a 14-year-old girl called Melinda. You are a gifted choreographer, and your daughter Melinda happens to have this same gift.

If you as the parent refuse to CULTIVATE your gift, and Melinda went ahead to CULTIVATE hers: learning, studying, practicing, doing research, attending choreography shows, dance shows, music concerts, and much more; what do you think would happen? Irrespective of her age, she would become an expert and perhaps grow to the point of becoming your instructor.

In fact, the mother may require paying to watch Melisa perform, even though she has this same gift of becoming an expert choreographer - though still in its undeveloped form. The parent, though having the potential to become successful like the child is stifled and their gift left dormant because of their unwillingness to stretch themselves.

This means that the parent's ability to become great at choreography is dependent on his or her willingness and desire to study, do research, learn, and practice: do everything that Melisa did to get to that point. This requires a great deal of commitment and dedication.

What sacrifices are you making, what commitments are you making to maximizing what you have been given?

I believe as you read this book, you've become aware of a potential you've left dormant. Raw talent doesn't make any impact. It's only that which has been refined and developed by you that can become useful.

## WHAT ARE YOU WAITING FOR?

Sometimes it may look like you are not making any progress. It might seem like you are even failing, and the future might look bleak. But if you will just persevere and be patient, keep working at it and do not give up, no matter the challenges.

Stick to your purpose and maintain a positive attitude in spite of difficulty, obstacles, or discouragement. Like the Bible says, put your hands in the plough and never look back. (*Luke 9:62*)

I like that word CULTIVATE, and to a great extent, our fulfilment and even prosperity are dependent on this word.

**To CULTIVATE means the following:**

1. To prepare and work on the land to raise crops
2. To promote or improve the growth of a plant, crop by labour and attention
3. To develop or improve oneself through education or training

> "And the Lord God took the man and put him into the garden of Eden to dress it and to keep it."
>
> **- Genesis 2:15**

**Eden** - in the original Hebrew translation means - '*A place of delight, pleasure, gentle; A state of happiness and bliss.*

So, my thought then is; if Eden is a place of delight, pleasure, and so gentle, it seems to me as a perfect handwork of the Creator? Why then was Adam required to do anything else about it?

If God has put Adam in this place of pleasure, why does he have to work on it? If I have been apportioned a place of delight, I would imagine no further work should be required.

Genesis 2:7-8 makes us understand that,

> "The time came when the Lord God formed a man's body from the dust of the ground and breathed into it the breath of life. And man became a living person. Then the Lord God planted a garden in Eden, to the east, and placed in the garden the man he had formed."

Although Adam was placed in the garden, purpose, and definition was not yet given to his placement or positioning, until Genesis 2:15, "…….To dress it and to keep it."

Pause for a moment and say these words to yourself, "Do some work" "Dress it and keep it."

The word **'DRESS'** means the following:

- To cut up, trim, and remove the skin, feathers, viscera,
- To prepare (skins, fabrics, timber, stone, ore, etc.) by special processes.

God was building in man the mindset that things are not meant to be left on their own, but to be evaluated, improved on, or **CULTIVATED**. So, considering this, the plants of nature, left to their own course, may degenerate and become wild through the poverty of the soil, or the gradual exhaustion of once rich soil.

This is indicative that when we don't discover, develop, and utilize our gifts, skills, or even opportunities God has given us, they can begin to decline or deteriorate.

## OUR HANDS HAVE BEEN BLESSED TO DRESS AND KEEP OUR GARDEN

The *"keeping"* of the garden may refer to the protection of it by enclosure from the plunders of the cattle, the wild beasts, or even the smaller animals. It also includes the faithful preservation of it as a trust committed to man by his generous Maker.

So, we are looking at how God made one man and gave him the responsibility of dressing and keeping the garden – The Abundance of One.

Did God, the maker of all flesh, not have the power to create so many people at that one time to look after the garden? It could have made the work easier and faster.

I remember making reference to this;

Take an example from the Royal family here in the United Kingdom. Every son born in that lineage is born a Prince, with the Potential of becoming a king someday, no matter when.

That said, they do not leave their development of becoming a king to chance. They make a carefully chosen and thoughtfully organized plan to ensure they are prepared to assume the throne whenever the need arises.

You must consciously decide to cultivate your intrinsic kingly ability or potential. When you do this, a shift will occur in your life that will bring transformation and position you for greatness.

Contrary to how Proverbs 22:29 has been perceived, a question was asked, and it was accompanied by a corresponding response:

> "Do you see someone skilled in their work? They will serve before kings; they will not serve before officials of low rank."

I like the fact that the response was not circumstantial but almost definite, showing some certainty – *"They will stand before Kings."* But this assurance is depended on the skill of the individual and the diligence of the diligent.

This is how The Passion Translation (TPT) illustrates Proverbs 22:29:

> "If you are uniquely gifted in your work, you will rise and be promoted. You won't be held back - you'll stand before kings!"

Therefore, when you decide to cultivate the king in you, you will eventually become what you have been designed to be.

The reason why most of us have remained in one spot over the years and appear powerless is not that the devil has tremendous power. Rather it's because we haven't cultivated our kingly ability from within. We haven't decided to shift things.

Becoming has less to do with what you do but your commitment to self-manifestation. Some of us just have to keep showing up and keep cutting that tree on that one spot.

## What is really stopping you?

Have you heard the voice of your heart speak louder than the doubts in your head? Do you know how it feels when you discover deep down, that you've found the answer everyone is looking for? How about when you realize that your excitement has been short-circuited, knowing that your ideas are not adequate to solve the existing problem? Have you ever felt the fear and uncertainty that clouds the mind just after you experience embarrassing failure because you dared to try that once 'golden' idea?

Do you believe in God's ability to place information, ideas, opportunities, inklings, and innovations in your heart? Have you ever linked God's blessings with divine information, creative ideas, open doors of opportunities, and strategic breakthrough in your mind?

Do you have ONE idea? Are you anxious and worried, feeling inadequate because it looks too small, too insignificant, and so insufficient? What if you were told that what is planted in you is ONE idea, placed in your care, and positioned in your life to change your world?

Have you considered the power of just ONE seed, ONE idea, ONE family, ONE leader, ONE vote? What about ONE penny, ONE place, ONE man, ONE mission, ONE dream, ONE day, or ONE assignment?

To begin with, I want to let you know that a lot of people want many things, more opportunities, an easier journey through life, several material things to feel happier, and more ways to get busy to drown the inner voice that craves for meaning and fulfilment.

It is important to note that sometimes it is not in the multiples of tasks, ideas, visions, jobs, careers, talents, and opportunities that you find fulfilment and real purpose for living. There could just be that ONE thing that when it is focused on, nurtured and activated can bring fulfilment and success in life

Therefore, I welcome you to the first chapter of this phenomenal book, it is time to discover that ONE thing that has been strategically planted into your heart and divinely placed on your hands to launch you into a new realm of ABUNDANCE.

Before you complain about how life has been so unfair to you, why don't you take time out to look within and find that ONE thing that you have probably set aside and underutilized? God is ever faithful and kind, He never leaves us without at least ONE way to rise above our limitations to a place of fulfilment, prominence, and prosperity.

After all, the problem is that often, we are running to do other things, polarizing our focus and undermining the golden opportunity that has been provided for us.

## AMAZON: ONE MAN, ONE IDEA

Let's take a cue from Amazon. The company is considered one of the Big Four technology companies today, along with Google, Apple, and Facebook. It is regarded as the world's largest internet company by revenue.

But the question is, has Amazon been always like this from the beginning? In reality, when Amazon started, there was no Prime delivery, no same-day delivery, neither was there any opportunity for you to order something online and then go to a collection point, put in your code, and collect what you've ordered, without any human assistance. None whatsoever.

There was nothing except that one man conceived one idea. He sat down, and over time through that, one idea created multiple channels that accentuates that one idea. He probably did not begin by opening several other businesses, maybe he did, but my point of emphasis is that ONE idea. He did not abandon the one idea and started chasing other things - this is one of the secrets of this global brand.

In the beginning, God created one Garden, one light, one river with multiple channels that flow into that same river, and then created one man into the Garden. And from that one man, we have the millions of people on earth today. That is the abundance of ONE.

Surprisingly, a lot of people today allow what they have done to limit the abundant potential in the one thing God has placed in them to emerge. Some are drowned in the well of self-pity. They keep wishing they can have more. While others wish they have more of what God has placed in their hand currently and so they keep waiting and searching for a more promising idea and innovation; while they already have with them and in them, the one idea needed to feed millions of people.

Take, for instance, one may say, "I lack the experience and expertise needed to manage such major cooperation" or "I don't have the financial base to even fertilize such idea." Hence, they starve the idea. Forgetting that in most cases, you don't necessarily have to personally manage the organization until it reaches a global status. In some cases, someone with business insight and a vast investment capacity can see the great potential in that idea you think is small, and fund it for you.

But this is not possible if you do not first see the potential in the ONE idea that you have.

## Count your blessing

Let's learn from the teaching of Jesus while he also requested that we count our blessings.

> *So, no one can become my disciple unless he first sits down and* **COUNTS HIS BLESSINGS..."**
> - Luke 14:25-33 (TLB)

This was Jesus rolling out certain conditions to be met for anyone that so desires to be his disciple. From this translation of the bible, he said such a person should count his blessing.

It's important to note that your blessing in this context refers to what you already have, the one thing you have been given, what you have at your disposal, in your control. Not counting what you hope to have, what you wish to have, or working towards having in the nearest future. The call is now, and so the valuation must be now. The counting of your blessing is symbolic of properly assessing what you have.

Jesus was expecting them to look inward at the resources they have at their disposal with regard to the commitment they were about to make? The all-knowing God was confident they have something needed for a walk with Him. And the beauty of all this is that Jesus was not placing a limit on what they should have or the quantity, all He needed them to do was to identify and acknowledge that they have something.

## FOCUS ON YOURSELF - AVOID COMPARISON

With all these in mind, the fact is, everyone has something. But the problem is either we have failed to identify it, or refuse to develop it, or perhaps we do not know how to maximize it. Whichever category you fall into, the fact still remains that God has not created anyone empty.

I agree with this saying that *"Don't compare yourself with others. You have no idea what their journey is all about"*.

From the parable of the talents, Jesus talked about a master who has three employees and gave them talents or resources:

> <sup>14</sup> "For it will be like a man going on a journey, who called his servants and entrusted to them his property. <sup>15</sup> To one, he gave five talents, to another two, to another one, to each according to his ability. Then he went away."
>
> **- Matthew 25:14-15**

From this illustration, we can deduce that perhaps not everyone can manage plenty to get plenty. Some are given multiple assignments with multiple expectations, whereas some are given just one thing that will also birth various outcomes.

A lot of times, we focus on another person's blessing and potential, and this attitude makes us despise our own. We have not taken the time to exhaust that one thing that we have. We have not finished working on that one thing that we have. We are running to do other things. Rather than nurture the one we have to full blossom.

**A parable of workers in the vineyard was cited in Matthew 20:1-16.**

In my understanding, this parable highlights the fact that God, the owner of everything, and maker of everyone, knows everyone's ability. He knows what we have the capacity for and delegates responsibilities to us in accordance with what we can handle.

The parable describes how workers were hired at different times within a day and yet were paid the same wages at the close of business.

While some may want to focus on the generosity of the business owner – Who I consider being God in this context, I would like to underline the understanding and business management skills of the business owner.

He, probably from experience, has identified that there are workers who have the skill, expertise, and tenacity to work from the opening of business to the close of business and achieve significant results.

But he also understands that certain skills may just be required to come in at the close of business when the project is at the closing stages: just to finish things up and still accomplish great results despite the time.

Also, for cost-effective purposes and perhaps office management reasons, it will not display a good business sense if everyone is brought in at the same time. For, everyone is given different talents, skills, and abilities. Everyone is utilized at different times and for various purposes. But ultimately, we are all given SOMETHING.

It behoves me, therefore, to encourage you to look inward. Quit looking at other people: the abundance in the one thing you have in your hand can become a reality.

Think about this!

Have you identified that one thing God has given you that has the potential of transforming your life?

# CHAPTER Two

## Start Before You Are Ready!

> "People will not be ASHAMED OF THE SMALL BEGINNINGS, and they will be very happy when they see Zerubbabel with the plumb line, measuring and checking the finished building. Now the seven sides of the stone you saw represent the eyes of the LORD looking in every direction. They see everything on earth."
>
> **- Zechariah 4:10**
> (Easy-to-Read Version)

I believe that one of the greatest threats to success is the fear of starting. The voices in our heads that keeps saying, "Are you ready for this?" "Are you good enough?" "Do I have what it takes?" "What if I make mistakes?" "What is the ABUNDANCE of ONE?"

Likewise, we often tell ourselves, "I don't have enough money to see this through, so I better wait for the next opportunity to invest." The mentality of thinking that something is "Not enough" has robbed many people of remarkable opportunities. In fact, many have become victims of stagnation, frustration, and depression just because they have chosen to remain by the shores of great opportunities, waiting for a BETTER time to get started.

Let's explore this chapter as it has the potential of causing a major mind-shift in your heart. Read carefully, and you will find strength and insight for your journey to ABUNDANCE. For, it is time to fuel your confidence so you can face those anxieties, concerns, fears, doubts, and worries that put you behind the shadows of self-sabotaging beliefs.

One of America's most successful authors, Steven Pressfield, said, *"The key to success is to get started before you are READY!"* What an incredible statement!

## START IN THE MIDST OF UNCERTAINTIES/ OVERCOME THE FEAR OF THE UNKNOWN

Alright, let's look into this. For the majority, it is invisible, it is the hidden challenge that lies between the known and the unknown that develops into fear and eventually stops us from the initiation stage. So, we conceived something, but the challenge of where we are and where we are headed cripples us and consequently immobilizes us.

An example is a scenario where God has told you that He would give you the nation of South Africa, and there you are in one little place, one village, one community, with few loved ones, trying to find your way out of that point. So, this is what God has shown you, but this is what you know. In many cases, if we are not careful, it is that hyphen between the known and the unknown as small as it is that cripples us.

## TIME IS VALUABLE

If you started yesterday, you would be a day ahead by now. Don't hesitate to begin! If you planted maize seed 3 days ago in your farmyard, it would have germinated by now. The more you wait to do that which you are meant to do, the more you will be unable to do it.

For the sake of guidance, let's consider the words of the wisest king, Solomon:

> "To everything, there is a season and a time to every purpose under the heaven."
> **- Ecclesiastes 3:1.**

There is time to plant, and that time is now. Don't rip yourself of your bountiful harvest because of fear and negligence. I think I need to shout this louder, you have all it takes, so start! It is in starting that you receive grace to finish. Stop praying for grace, start acting gracefully.

## START WITH THE RIGHT ATTITUDE

That you must not compromise is Gratitude. Thanksgiving creates the platform for unending favour.

When God created one man in the garden, he blessed him and said: "be fruitful and multiply." One of the ways to provoking multiplication of the ONE thing God has given you is to be grateful for it.

'For instance, When Jesus was faced with the challenge of feeding 5,000, the disciples had with them the ONE thing needed to feed the multitude, but they despised it.

The same meal that was despised, Jesus took it and gave thanks, and it multiplied. What you have in your hands will start multiplying when you pay attention to it and give thanks to God.

This principle of the multiplication of the bread and fishes is the principle of acknowledgment. That divine seed in your hands will not multiply except you start with gratitude.

The time will not always be right, you have to make it right. Decide to finish. Decide not to be moved by negative situations. Decide to be a success.

Nobody can make these crucial decisions for you. Only you can genuinely encourage yourself, especially at this starting stage. Don't compare yourself with someone else. The bible calls those who compare themselves with others fools.

> 'For we dare not make ourselves of the number, or compare ourselves with some that commend themselves: but they measuring themselves by themselves, and comparing themselves among themselves, are not wise.'
>
> **- 2 Corinthians 10:12**

The only competition you have is against yourself. The success or failure of another person is not the measuring rod for your success. You are only permitted to measure yourself against what God says you are. The seed you are endowed with is tailor-made for you. It is only you that has the configuration to successfully deliver the idea. Don't sell yourself short. Start with a conquering attitude, and you will conquer.

**Finally, you need to break free from your past so you can prepare for your future**

> "Behold, I will do a new thing; now it shall spring forth; shall ye not know it? I will even make a way in the wilderness and rivers in the desert."
>
> **- Isaiah 43:19**

One major challenge of starting is the thoughts and limitations of past failures. Most people bring a picture of their past into their current situation, and when it looks as though it does not fit in, they give up and fail to start eventually.

Did you have a rough past? Or did you come from a background that is too low compared to the height God has shown you? Each time you attempt to start you hear a voice telling you how you've failed in the past, whenever you want to make a move into something great, that mindset will come and say "you know you can't," "don't even go there" and before long you find yourself drawn back to the status quo of mediocrity as though God hasn't told you anything before.

For instance, God is instructing you to start a singles ministry, and each time you attempt the move, your mind is drawn, taking you to where you are passed, your weakness, and reminding you of your errors while you were single.

Well, you need to understand that there is nothing you can do to change your past. God is not judging you based on your past failures and defeats. He is more concerned about what you will do with what He has committed into your hand today.

There is a saying that *"Once your mindset changes, everything on the outside will change along with it."*

So quit pitying yourself, don't allow the devil to rob you of the joy of tomorrow. Develop the right mindset to success, victory, progress, advancement, and fulfilment of purpose. Be optimistic about the success of that idea and let it energize you to start.

Hear what the wise King Solomon said;

> "For as he thinks within himself, so he is. He says to you, "Eat and drink!" But his heart is not with you."
> **- Proverbs 23:7**
> (New American Standard Bible)

In other words, no man is different from his thought. So, you will be doing yourself a great good by letting go of your past and think positively about the future.

Finally. Solomon further advises that the best time to start is not when the weather is clear because it may never be clear anytime soon. But the best time to start is NOW.

> *"Farmers who wait for perfect weather never plant. If they watch every cloud, they never harvest."*
>
> **- Ecclesiastes 11:4**
> (New Living Translation)

But in other to prevent starting and falling, we shall examine some other principles needed to set you up for success in our next chapter.

# CHAPTER
## *Three*

## Set Yourself Up For Success

> "This Book of the Law shall not depart from your mouth, but you shall meditate on it day and night, so that you may be careful to do according to all that is written in it. For then you will make your way prosperous, and then you will have good success."
>
> **- Joshua 1:8**
> (English Standard Version)

Among other things, success seems to be one of the greatest desires of every individual. Are you a student seeking to impress Momma by graduating with the best grades? Are you married, craving for love, attention, and fulfilment in marriage? Do you desire to be awarded the most productive staff at the end of the company's financial year? Are you a business owner desiring to be ranked among the top-rated companies in the city?

Well, if your answer to any of these questions is YES, then, this alludes to the fact that the quest for success is part of your strongest desires. One more thing: there's nothing wrong with wanting to be successful, the challenge is, how can you set yourself up for success?

Do you realize that many people have sunk in the mire of constant depression, sense of emptiness, feelings of meaninglessness and lack of fulfilment just because they are always set up to be at the short end of the stick?

But the question is, have you ever done any project that didn't go as planned? Maybe you've ventured into a business, fully optimistic about the viability of such an investment, but in the long run, you can't even account for the capital anymore? Are you facing some challenges in your marriage, and you wish you had never said, "Yes, I do"? Or are you currently paying back a loan, and you constantly regret ever taking it up for that 'brilliant idea' in the first place?

If any of these sceneries applies to you in any way; then, make sure you read these lines very carefully. Because this chapter has been strategically included to provide a mental and spiritual backdrop for personal reflection as you diagnose the cause of the heart-wrenching failure.

The big question is: ARE YOU SET-UP FOR SUCCESS or failure?

Carefully think about it. Life is a field of waves of cause and effect. Far from an accident - success and failure are outcomes of decisions and positions that we take, especially before we set-out on the projects that matter to us.

It is time to find help to navigate situations, issues, and attitudes that have always hemmed you in behind the veil of failure. You will learn about the principles of success in almost all areas of life. Let's get started!

## FIRST, EXCITEMENT IS NOT ENOUGH!

In the previous chapter, you were encouraged to START BEFORE YOU ARE READY! Now, you may wonder why excitement about starting your project is not enough to guarantee success. Here it is.

You see, excitement may fuel action and inspire attitude, yet, they don't guarantee success. In life, so many people have taken some important decisions just because they felt so excited about the process or envisaged outcome. This is not a problem when your feelings are contained within appropriate and sufficient considerations.

Notwithstanding, when you allow your emotions to shield you away from obvious realities, you may **not** be set-up for your desired outcome. Reality can be ignored, but ignorance doesn't change reality. The fact that you were thrilled, emotionally excited, and enthusiastic about that project, business idea, oversea investment, love relationship, and big opportunity does not bring you to the end of the road. It's just the beginning, a call to wait, sit back, and consider your options, decisions, and possible outcomes.

You need to consider the flip side. How about asking further questions and thinking through your decisions? So, if the emotion is not enough, what then am I missing?

## WHY NOT SIT DOWN, COUNT, AND THINK BEFORE YOU START?

Therefore, rather than being carried away with the excitement and prospect in your next step, why not take a sit and think through. This is an important step in setting yourself up for success in any area of life. However, setting off before sitting down has ended many great and potentially huge ideas before they even started. We often find out that most people are too much in a hurry to start and then miss that vital opportunity to first SIT. When an exciting idea comes to their mind, they zoom off to do all kinds of stuff, rather than first sit down to think about the idea and mentally process it.

> *"Be still, and know that I am God…"*
> **- Psalm 46:10**

Psalm 46:10 highlights the knowledge that is derived from observing a still position – 'Be still, and know that I am God.' There is so much power in staying still to secure a right perspective about your project. We live in a world filled with so many noises, distractions, sounds, and speed without focus, awareness, and direction for success.

To "SIT DOWN" means you are taking a strategic position where you can inquire into an issue or assess your situation. In this position, or at this stage, you can ask questions, analyse the options, and logically examine the possible outcomes.

Also, you can think carefully about the matter at hand, especially before making very important decisions. Taking an emotional perspective without thinking objectively may present only the positive outcomes in your decision and can easily blindside you. But taking time to think helps you see the reverse. And you get to assess your assets and make an informed decision if you have what it takes to go through with the idea.

Furthermore, when you sit down and think, it allows you to carefully examine your idea and objectively check its viability. You explore, investigate, scrutinize, and examine carefully before making commitments.

Also, sitting down to think also helps you to look within and count the cost to know if you have sufficient resources to undertake the task.

It's important to state here that actions or decisions that come after sitting down and thinking through a matter are premeditated, deliberate, planned, and purposeful rather than left to chance.

Do you want to learn something helpful? Before you join that organization, start that business, embark on that bag-packing journey, relocate to the seemingly greener pasture, have you taken the time to sit down, think and count the cost?

Have you checked your resources against the demands of that new location, or are you only excited about the prospect of relocating? Have you taken the time to consider the associated cost of running the business for a year, or are you just excited about the prospect of a trial profit?

Sit, Think, and Count must be your starting mantra. They must become the veritable actions and attitudes that set you up for success. When you ignore these important steps, you have done yourself so much disservice.

Therefore, you don't need to be surprised when you encounter daunting challenges and unexpected bumps on the road to success. All you need is to ensure that you had not failed before you even started just because you failed to sit-down and refused to count the cost.

Consider the scriptures as referenced in the previous chapter. The Bible says,

> *"But don't begin until you COUNT THE COST. For who would begin construction of a building without first getting estimates and then checking to see if he has enough money to pay the bills? 29 Otherwise, he might complete only the foundation before running out of funds. And then how everyone would laugh!"*
>
> **- Luke 14:28-29**
> (New Living Translation)

Jesus gave two scenarios to describe the condition to be his follower. He talked about a man that needed to build. He explained that the man will first sit and think if he has enough to finish the building even before starting. So, he won't be a laughing stock. He also referred to another man going to battle, he must first think if he is strong enough to win the war, better still he should seek peace.

This was what Jesus was talking about; Do not get carried away with the excitement and prospect of becoming a follower, or in this case, living your dreams without having to sit down, think and count your blessing, critically analysing what resources you have, or can lay hold of.

He illustrated the necessity of deliberately weighing your idea against your available resources: whether you are able and prepared to stick your neck out, take on a project that has the potential to attract ridicule if you are unable to complete it.

## THINK AND PRAY

Do you know the power of prayer? Even more, how about the possibility of thinking and praying? Have you ever experienced the power that is released when you think through the issues in your life and then turn to God in prayer?

Well, one thing a lot of Christians don't understand is the power of the mind. We fail to realize that siting to think will eventually help your prayers to flow from a more guided heart and brightly illuminated soul.

Most times, we run off and start praying without X-raying our heart's desires and personal requests. We need to take time to reflect and think over the things we are about to bring before God in prayer. As much as I appreciate speaking to God, I also believe in the power of thinking-through with God for the desired breakthrough.

We understand the importance of reasoning from Isaiah. In Isaiah 1:18, God made this remarkable statement;

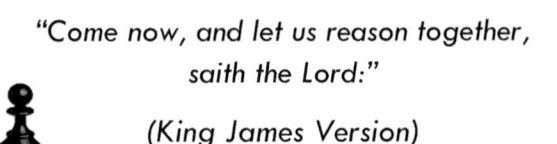

> "Come now, and let us reason together, saith the Lord:"
>
> (King James Version)

But the Expanded Bible version gives a clearer perspective of that same verse, it says:

> The Lord says, "Come, let us ·talk about these things [reason together; or settle this matter; or consider your options]

Even though prayer is communication with God, yet, at times, we just talk and don't wait for a response from God. This is not communication.

Do you think before you pray? Have you realized that thinking before praying can enable you to have more questions that you can ask in prayers?

I believe that the more we exercise the mind before engaging our tongue, the more we are likely to wait for answers from the presence of God. The truth is God desires that we reason with Him before, during, and after prayers.

Listen to what God is saying to you and me.

> "Come now, let us reason together, says the LORD..."
>
> **- Isaiah 1:18**
> (English Standard Version)

## LESSONS FROM KING DAVID

David was one of the wisest and most powerful Kings in Israel. He was a man who knew the power of the mind, the place of numbers, and the influence of prayers.

In 1 Samuel chapter 30, the bible said when David and his men came back from the battle, they discovered that their wives, their children, homes, and goods had been plundered.

Here is the way it was described:

> "And David was greatly distressed, for the people spoke of stoning him, because all the people were bitter in soul, each for his sons and daughters. But David strengthened himself in the LORD his God."

Now notice that David and his men were in the same precarious situation. But there was a difference in the way David responded. While others resorted to violence, David harnessed his emotion. He refused to allow his emotion to ride away with him.

David was able to set himself for success by taking control of his mind. This brought him in a position where he was able to leverage the power of a still and calm mind even in the storms of life.

The Bible said David encouraged himself in the Lord. It shows that we need to get help for our minds in times of troubles and unpleasant surprises. We need an anchor for our souls.

## GOD CAN HELP YOU ARRIVE AT THE ANSWERS YOU SEEK

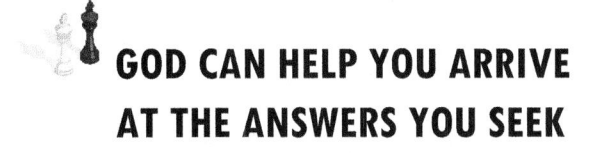

> *⁷ And David said to Abiathar the priest, the son of Ahimelech, "Bring me the ephod." So Abiathar brought the ephod to David.*

Notice that the word "INQUIRED" as used in the scriptures means, David didn't go blank as he reached out to God. He went with questions and ideas of what he intended to do to get his family back.

Interestingly, David asked God very clear and critical questions. He said, "Shall I pursue which means, should I go after my adversaries?"

Notice, David won't have come up with those ideas without first moving away from the people who were too busy crying more than they could think through the current challenge.

Eventually, God gave David the green light because he was ready to move. That is how effective our prayers can be when we learn to think before praying.

It can be said that thinking takes time and energy, yet it remains the missing link for most people. They hurry in and hurry out. They run with the fuel of feelings and excitements, running without direction and navigating life without discretion, thereby setting themselves up for failure.

Having said that, you don't have to go like others have gone, you must stand ready to ignore the fact that even though you may appear slow and sluggish, your focus should be a lasting legacy, not just transient success.

## REACH OUT FOR INSIGHT

Become like David and reach out for insight about that situation. David wanted to know the mind of God about the things he was going through. David was not just concerned about speaking empty words and complaining to God about his predicament.

Rather, he was interested in feeding his mind with insight about the way forward. He presented his thoughts on the matter to God. His questions were not vain, empty, and baseless. He said, "shall I pursue this raiding party? Will I overtake them?" And God's response surprisingly corresponded with the thoughts David had put forward, and even more.

God said, "Pursue them, he answered. You will certainly overtake them and succeed in the rescue". (I Samuel 30:8-9). Why not set out with this same attitude of going to the Lord with thoughts, ideas, or reason.

At this point, I need to stress that I'm not elevating the mind above God. Instead, I'm helping you to realize the vantage point that can be secured when you engage and align your mind with God.

David was not just sitting dejectedly somewhere, thinking about how unfair life has been; rather, he was in close communion with God and His Word for his desired result.

Finally, David was successful because He had set himself for success right from the start. The Bible says:

> *And there was nothing lacking to them, neither small nor great, neither sons nor daughters, neither spoil nor anything that they had taken to them: DAVID RECOVERED ALL."*
>
> **- 1 Samuel 30: 6-19**

# CHAPTER

## *Four*

### When One Feels Like None

> *"Do not try to do everything.*
> *Do one thing well."*
>
> **- Steve Jobs**

Have you ever seen the size of a fully-grown oak tree? It's huge! Oak trees grow most times, to be about forty-five meters tall and over forty meters wide. On the other hand, have you seen the seed of an Oak tree? It's also known as an Oak-nut or acorn. They are pretty small, about 1-6cm long. Yet one little acorn grows into a massive Oak tree and can produce more than a million seeds in its lifetime. Isn't this amazing that just one seed can become so abundant?

It's the same with human life. Abundance is first, one seed before the massive Oak. Most times, we get stuck in a place where one feels like none. The *never-enough* mentality has to leave before we can manifest the kind of abundance that we're destined for.

The truth is, we're expected to be just like that little seed. We must invest, cultivate, or trade-in that one thing we have to get what we want-- abundance. It begins with an understanding that one is never too little. You'll always have just enough to become fruitful and multiply. Get ready to learn to maximize that **one-thing** in your life even if it seems like all you've got.

Now, no matter how little your potential or resources seem, if you can master the art of making the most of little, the sky won't be your limit but your starting point.

A business influencer once said, "*It's easier to know what to do with $1,000,000 than to wisely invest $100.*" And this is the reason so many people remain in lack, even when they have resources that can yield fruit and give them the life of their dreams, they don't know what to do with it.

But with the right information and wisdom, you can turn your $10 to $100. It all starts with knowing what is available to you, cherishing it, and identifying the people or places you can strategically invest it.

Let's look at some excellent examples of people who had nothing but one thing in life. They were utterly disadvantaged but learned how to transform their little into much and their one into abundance.

## LINCOLN'S ONE

Abraham Lincoln was born into a low-income family and was raised on the frontiers in Indiana. His father was a farmer and a carpenter, and his mother died when he was only nine years old. Lincoln's chances for a better future were slim. He never got a formal education because his father couldn't afford it.

Indeed, young Abraham Lincoln lacked the privileges most children had. Nonetheless, he had one thing. Before her death, His mother, Nancy Hanks Lincoln, had instilled in the little boy love and curiosity for knowledge. Despite all the other things he didn't have, Lincoln has this intense desire to learn.

He maximized this one-thing he had, and soon he became a lawyer, a U.S Congressman, and the sixteenth President of the United States. And these things were possible because he recognized that his knack for learning was his one-thing (His seed), so he planted it by educating himself. He read everything he could lay his hands on until he made it to the oval office.

On the other hand, imagine if Abe had given up on his future because life didn't give him enough to work with. What if he had treated his one like it was none? He probably wouldn't have become one of the greatest Presidents America ever had.

## SOMETHING OUT OF NOTHING

Frederick Douglas was born into slavery. At an early age, he was separated from his mother, and he never knew his father. His life was characterized by cruelty, pain, maltreatment, and other evils slaves had to confront daily. He lived in an era where slaves were treated like animals. They made sounds but had no voice, and they had faces without identity.

This little boy had nothing to look forward to; there was no light at the end of the tunnel. He had no family, no education, and no prospects. Most people have loved ones and friends that can support them; Douglas was all alone.

But he found hope where they seemed to be none. Life had given him one thing: a sound mind. So, Douglas invested in his mind by teaching himself to read and write.

He would secretly collect newspapers and books because his master believed that slaves shouldn't be educated. He said it was equivalent to freedom.

Later in life, he would say, "Knowledge is the pathway from slavery to freedom." As time passed, Frederick Douglas began to teach other slaves how to read and write. He went on to become a social reformer, abolitionist, orator, writer, and statesman. He's another person who recognized his one-thing and turned it into abundance.

## WHAT'S YOUR *ONE*?

Take a minute to reflect on your life. What do you have that so little? What have you despised because it didn't look promising? Did you close your business after a month of opening it because it wasn't receiving enough patronage? Of maybe you lost a job, and it feels like it's the end of the world?

Well, can you restructure your thinking? What's in your hand? Is there a bright side to your dark situation? What's that one thing that feels like none? Yes, you lost your job, but at least you still have an apartment? You can turn your house into an office! And probably you got a divorce, but you still have your kids; build a strong relationship with them.

In other words, amid the hopelessness in your life, there still one thing of value. Indeed, there's always a remnant, but it may feel like nothing-like mere scrap. On the contrary, that one thing that's left in your life is your ticket to abundance.

## THE MAN WHO BURIED ABUNDANCE

There's an interesting story in the Bible that teaches the importance of maximizing little. It's a typical example of having one thing that can produce the greatness you desire and yet treating it like garbage.

In Matthew 25:16-29, Jesus told a parable of a man who, having to go on a business trip, left his servants in charge of his property. This man gave his three servants talents (Hebrew money in the form of gold coins) for profitable ventures. The talents were apportioned according to each one's ability—their capacity to be fruitful and multiply, despite challenges. He gave the first servant five talents, the second servant two talents, and he gave the third servant one talent.

Just a moment, while you consider the three servants, I want you to think a little about the disparity in the distribution modality. It's easy to be happy when you're getting five talents. What if you were a musical prodigy, a mathematical genius, a professional ice-skater, and had the artistic skills of Picasso? That's four incredible abilities. Won't life be amazing? What if you had just one?

Well, whatever you're given, you'll be asked to account for it. The Bible says that, to whom much is given, much is expected (Luke 12:48). God is an investor and expects us to maximize our resources--no matter how insignificant it may seem—to produce abundance. So, the question isn't if you have much, it's if you can produce much from little.

Let's get back to the story. After distributing the talents, the master went on his trip, which lasted several days. Immediately he left, His servants swung into action:

> "...he that had received the five talents went and traded with the same, and made them other five talents. And likewise, he that had received two, he also gained other two. But he that had received one went and dug in the earth, and hid his Lord's money."
>
> **- Matthew 25:16-18**

Now, from the scripture above, it is clear that of the three servants, only two efficiently put their money to work to produce abundance. The servant who had five talents doubled his money, and so did the one with two talents.

In contrast, the servant with one talent gone nothing in return. Was it because one is too small an amount to produce anything? Definitely not! He didn't get an increase in his talents because he didn't put it to work. While the other servants traded with their resources, this servant buried his one talent.

There's a profound truth in this story: one can become abundant if you trade with it. On the other hand, if you despise it and treat it as nothing, it won't yield any fruit. Similarly, this unwise servant got nothing in return because he despised what he got.

Right now, is there anything or situation in your life you despise? Do you hate your job because it's not what you wanted? Do you despise your marriage? Wait a minute, don't bury what is not yet dead. If only you can put your one-thing to work, it'll give you the increase you desire.

## YOU'LL ACCOUNT FOR ONE

> "After a long time, the lord of those servants returned and settled accounts with them."
> **- Matthew 25:19**

After a long while, the master who had left his servants in charge of his property returned. When he finally settled down from his long journey, he invited his servants to come before him and present their records. Each one of them was to give a detailed account of how they used what he'd given them.

Matthew 25:20-31 made it clear that the master wasn't just interested in balancing his records, but also desired to reward those who had maximized their resources. He was pleased with the other two servants who had done something with their talents. They were described as good and faithful servants, and he committed more to them because they had proven that they could produce abundance. But he was displeased with the servant who had buried his talent.

Although this servant had given excuses for not maximizing what was given to him, he had buried potential. Is there a good reason for that? His actions were described as wickedness and laziness because he had privileges and advantages most people didn't have. At least he had one talent that he could have utilized. Meanwhile, other people have no talent or resources available to them.

Imagine the tragedy of burying an idea that can create a multi-million-dollar business. What if Bill Gates had thrown the Microsoft-concept out the window of carelessness? So many people are neglecting international business ideas, best-selling books, ground-breaking inventions, and more unimaginable potentials.

Finally, remember the oak nut, small and fitting for a child's palm; it didn't look like much, yet consider what it's capable of becoming—a mighty Oaktree. Likewise, that one thing in your life is your abundance in disguise. But this can only become profitable when you stop seeing it as none and start maximizing it from an abundance perspective.

# CHAPTER
## *Five*

## The Multiplier Effect

> "Therefore, from one man, and him as good as dead, were born descendants as many as the stars of heaven and as many as the innumerable grains of sand by the seashore."
>
> **- Hebrews 11:12** (English Standard

*I*n all ages, survival usually depends on multiplying one to secure an abundance. You can see this truth play out in nature, especially among animals. Some species become extinct or face extinction because they don't multiply as much as required for perpetuity in the eco-system. They would have survived if they could reproduce faster and in larger numbers.

In truth, if not for multiplication, animals like the rabbit would have become extinct a long time ago. This is because fifteen percent of rabbit babies do not live longer than a year. They have an incredibly low survival rate. Yet, they still exist in enormous numbers because of their high reproductive rate, short gestation period, and rapid sexual maturity. They thrive by multiplying.

Likewise, everything that must survive and thrive in life must multiply. However, although rabbits multiply in large numbers as a default, you will have to be deliberate in other to have a multiplier effect. I mean, deliberate with that one thing in your possession; deliberate with your capital; deliberate your business.

Some businesses became household names and gained international recognition because they were deliberate about expansion and multiplication. One of the ways they achieved this was to establish a franchise. Also, there were world-changing and history-making ventures that utilized the strategy of franchising and became irreversibly successful.

According to Investopedia, "*A franchise is a type of license that a party (franchisee) acquires to allow them to have access to a business's (franchisor) proprietary knowledge, processes, and trademarks to allow the party to sell a product or provide a service under the business's name.*"

## MCDONALD'S FRANCHISE

Have you heard of McDonald's? McDonald's is an American fast-food company founded in 1940 as a restaurant operated by Richard and Maurice McDonald in San Bernardino, California, United States. They rechristened their business as a **hamburger stand**. They later turned the company into a franchise, with the Golden Arches logo being introduced in 1953 at a location in Phoenix, Arizona.

In 1955, Ray Kroc, a businessman, joined the company as a franchise agent and proceeded to purchase the chain from the McDonald brothers.

McDonald's used the strategy of a franchise in sustaining their company and giving it the financial boost, it needed. Your franchisee bears your name, your reputation, and your trademarks. Franchising is like marketing your integrity for another group of companies to leverage on.

Even though it was a risky adventure, it produced excellent results some years after—becoming a significant source of revenue. The effect of the McDonald's Corporation revenues come from the rent, royalties, and fees paid by the franchisees, as well as sales in company-operated restaurants.

Here are brothers who took their idea and developed it into something great. They were deliberate about turning their *one* into abundance. What about you? Have you been dreaming too little? Do you expect your business, career, or income to yield increase without being strategic and deliberate? Well, friend, multiplication is an effect. And you must create it by exchange and sacrifice.

## FAITH FRANCHISE

After God created the earth, He gave humanity a mandate in Genesis 1:28,

> *"And God blessed them, and God said unto them, Be fruitful, and multiply, and fill the earth, and subdue it: and have dominion over the fish of the sea, and over the fowl of the air, and over every living thing that moves upon the earth."*

God desired to multiply His nature and glory in the earth. Yes, heaven already reflected His perfection and splendour. But God wanted to create a multiplier effect that would bring heaven on earth. He planned to fill the world with people with thought and behaved like Him. So, He created man in His image and likeness. To God, this was real dominion.

However, this plan was aborted when man sinned and corrupted his nature. Instead of reflecting God's glory and beauty, the man expressed traits of sin and chaos. Consequently, God had to establish a new system through which his purpose will be accomplished.

Thus, God established a faith franchise to destroy the franchise of sin that Adam and Eve had begun. He appeared to Abraham to make him a father of many nations that through Abraham's seed, all the nations of the world would be blessed. He was going to restore His nature to humanity by making a sacrifice that would create a multiplier effect.

Since God wanted sons, He had to sow His son, Jesus, like a seed. And right from Abraham, to Moses and the Prophets, He began to set the stage for the establishment of a faith franchise. And when Jesus came to make this transaction after thousands of years, He revealed this truth to his disciples.

John 2:24 says, *"Verily, verily, I say unto you, Except a corn of wheat fall into the ground and die, it abideth alone: but if it dies, it bringeth forth much fruit."*

Jesus wasn't merely talking about crops and their ability to yield; he was referring to His death. He was this corn of wheat that was to be buried in the ground, and the fruit was the many sons and daughters that would come from the transaction through faith.

> "And that he died for all, that they which live **should not henceforth live unto themselves,** but unto **him which died for them,** **and rose again."**
> **- 2 Corinthians 5:15**

God exchanged Jesus to have the whole world restored to Himself. Think about the passage above. It says, 'and that He died for **all**...' He died for **all** -- just like a seed cast into the ground. The seed may look like a waste of investment but give it some time, and from it, you will reap the benefits of strategic exchange.

Why do you think a seed is left to die? It is for the sake of the **ALL** that a seed must die. Do you understand that? What is your seed that must die for the sake of your *all* to come?

God, a strategist, saw you and me in Him—Jesus! He saw the fruits that will proceed out of Jesus, so He made the massive investment of His son — Jesus. The profit of Jesus' death was the increase it brought to God.

Through Jesus, God received so many sons and daughters, establishing His plan of expressing His nature and glory in the world. In addition, God also multiplied His kingdom. Before Jesus died, God's kingdom was only in heaven. However, after this strategic transaction, the kingdom of God was present in every part of the world. No wonder Jesus made this profound statement, in Luke 17: 21, "nor will people say, 'Here is it,' or 'There it is,' because **the kingdom of God is in you**r midst."

God turned His kingdom business into a franchise on the day of Pentecost. He sent his Holy Spirit as a seal of ownership and commissioned them as His representatives. Not only that, but these ambassadors also bring a constant harvest of souls to the kingdom business of God.

What an excellent investment. See Ephesians 1:13, *"In whom ye also trusted, after that,* **ye heard the word of truth,** *the gospel of* **your**

***salvation:*** *in whom also after that **ye believed,** ye were **sealed with that Holy Spirit of promise,***"

Finally, having looked at a business franchise and a spiritual franchise, it is indisputable that multiplication doesn't just happen. There has to be a strategic plan to exchange or utilized one-thing to create abundance. McDonald's did this and their brand multiplied and gained international presence.

In the same vein, God worked out His great plan of salvation, and through Jesus, many men and women can become children of God and citizens of His kingdom. Jesus's death created the multiplier effect that fulfilled God's plan of redemption. What's your multiplier effect?

# CHAPTER Six

## Nurturing Your Dream

> "Now Joseph had a dream, and when he told it to his brothers ..."
> 
> **- Genesis 37:5**
> (English Standard Version)

A Dream is one of your greatest assets in life. Now, I'm not talking about the drama that plays out in your sleep. No! Life dreams don't need comfy pillows and long hibernation. You can catch a picture of the future with your eyes wide open and your mind sharply focused.

It's a blessing to realize that, like talents for everyone, dreams come to us all. It may be one, two, or five, in life, all that matter is finding the courage to nurture your dreams. So, whether you're born with a silver spoon, or you were raised without privileges, your dream can guarantee an equal chance at success in life.

How many dreams do you need to become successful? The answer is just one or a million dreams! You don't have to feel hopeless because all you have is just one dream. You see, in that one dream, you'll find all you can ever wish for.

Since the glory of gold points back to its refining process, so is the glitter of success pointing back to sacrifices of nurturing a dream. Therefore, a dream you refuse to nurture will remain an illusion or even become a nightmare.

So, how can anyone maximize today if they lack vision for tomorrow? Life is filled with many challenges, setbacks, and limitations—enough to stop anyone except the visionary. This is why dreams are powerful! Dreams bear the light of hope for tomorrow; with them, you can find the courage to rise and glow every morning, no matter the limits of your present reality.

## MLK:
## THE MAN WHO HAD BEEN TO THE FUTURE:

> "*I have a dream* that my four little children will one day live in a nation where they will not be judged by the colour of their skin but the content of their character.
> **I have a dream** today.
>
> **I have a dream** that one day every valley shall be exalted, every hill and mountain shall be made low, the rough places will be made plain, and every crooked place will be made straight, and the glory of the Lord shall be revealed, and all flesh shall see it together."

These were the words of the Nobel Peace award winner, Martin Luther King Jr., in a public speech he delivered during the *March on Washington for Job and Freedom* on the 28th of August, 1963. This mass rally was one that announced the heartbeat of the man behind the peaceful revolution. It broke the chains of oppression and segregation, not only for black Americans but all minorities and disadvantaged Americans.

Born in an era of social, economic, political, and racial discrimination in the modern, post-emancipation era, Martin Luther King, Jnr captured a dream. This became the foundational force of transformation in his life and countless others for generations to come.

In all ages, change is never easy. Luther was arrested over twenty times for leading peaceful protests against the inhumane and oppressive institution of his day. He witnessed several violent attacks, he was stabbed, and his house was set on fire. But Luther never gave up. And finally, his life was cut short on the altar of sacrifice-- a sacrifice for racial equality-- a sacrifice for a dream that continues to shape American reality.

Although, Martin Luther Jnr. was assassinated before all his dream came to pass, yet, his dream lived on. Dreams are immortal forces, even in the heart of mortal men. MLK had a dream that he nurtured under the weight of persecution and attacks— and eventually, it paid off.

Nurturing entails feeding, protecting, supporting, and encouraging something or someone during their season of training or development. Can you name anything or anyone who can thrive or even survive without nurture? Life without nurture is like new-borns without the loving arms of their mother and the protective shield of their father. Even a garden without a gardener will be wasted, while sheep would perish without their shepherd.

A dream without nurture is merely an illusion. Without enduring action, vision becomes blurry. Today, MLK lives on in the memory of many not just because he dreamed, but because he nurtured his dream into generational reality.

## YOU HAVE A DREAM EVEN IF YOU AREN'T MLK

I was fascinated by a YouTube video about an interesting phenomenon-- the *imposter syndrome.* The narrator described this syndrome as that silent noise in your head that continuously renders you as always inferior to other people, who you naturally idealize as life's worthy heroes. This comparison and mental clutter put you in the place of an imposter on the platform of great achievements and among great achievers.

While aiming a basketball to the net, the imposter syndrome would say: "You'll never be as good as Michael Jordan."

When you try to give a speech, it says, "You aren't MLK." While you run with colleagues, it screams, "Joe is the best in Math, he deserves to win this race, and you don't." Now, what's the relationship between calculus and marathon? This is the imposter's syndrome.

You need to discover the abundance in one. Even if it's one dream, one vision, one talent, or just you—you deserve abundance. The problem with an imposter's syndrome is how it kills your drive. You can only nurture what you value--what you are passionate about.

Nurturing a dream is not just for world leaders, Olympic athletes, or Forbes influencers. You also have a dream, worth realizing—a vision worth living for. Whether you desire to become a better student, successful entrepreneur, loving spouse, helpful friend, or even a healthier individual, I dare to say your dreams are legitimate.

It takes a shift in your mind about the power of a dream to change your life forever. It's easy to cast aside the pictures in your mind about the future. It feels intangible. Some may prefer a million dollars to a million dreams. Would you?

Unlocking a mentality for maximizing your life begins with recognizing the abundance of one, little, tiny, but personal dream. When you own your dream, it eventually owns you and moves you to the future few can only imagine.

You don't have to live on, tied within the plot of another man's dreams, except your dreams can thrive in the vineyard of their vision. You are the main character, the protagonist of your own dream—act like it!

Many are bowed down under the cloak of dogma and mundane expectations. Very few dares to step out and step up. You deserve the happiness of adventure and the fulfilment of accomplishments. But, until you nurture your dreams, who will? The remaining part of this chapter will break this down for you to understand.

To help you discover how dreams change lives. I want to show you some powerful lessons in the life of Joseph. Have you ever heard the name, Joseph? If you know any biblical and historical record of his life, you will agree that dreams played a vital role in Joseph's success story.

I was excited to find out that 'Joseph' is a Hebrew name for **"increase."** Indeed, names are powerful! But what's in a name? Joseph experienced an increase at every level and in every phase of his life. What was his secret? Just the name?

Born to Ol' Jacob by Racheal after many years of bareness, Joseph became motherless while Racheal was giving birth to her second child, Benjamin. Life would have been bearable if Joseph had only Benjamin to compete with, but life among ten older and nasty brothers was hell next door.

Fortunately, Joseph, like every man and woman, had one advantage. He was Papa Jacob's favourite among twelve sons. So, this meant that Joseph enjoyed immunity, preference, and first place with Jacob. While these felt like enough, Joseph found something more fascinating—dreams. He would stop at nothing to capture and tell dreams that towered above the status quo and the ambient negative energy of his home.

But what was Joseph's *unacceptable* dream all about? The Bible says,

> *7 There we were, binding sheaves in the field. Then behold, my sheaf arose and also stood upright; and indeed, your sheaves stood all around and bowed down to my sheaf.*
> **- Genesis 37:6-7**
> (New King James Version)

Obviously, Joseph's dreams were more important to him than his fear of rejection, hatred, and envy. Genesis Chapter 37 verses 8 reveals that,

> "And his brothers said to him,
> "Shall you indeed reign over us? Or shall you indeed have dominion over us?"
> So, they hated him even more for his dreams and for his words."

Now observe and note the question from Joseph's brothers, **"shalt thou indeed have dominion over us?"**

Likewise, hearing Jacob's response will help you grasp another essential truth.

> *⁹ Then he dreamed still another dream and told it to his brothers, and said, "Look, I have dreamed another dream. And this time, the sun, the moon, and the eleven stars bowed down to me."*
>
> *¹⁰ So he told it to his father and his brothers; and his father rebuked him and said to him, "What is this dream that you have dreamed? Shall your mother and I and your brothers indeed come to bow down to the earth before you?"*
>
> **- Genesis 37:9-10**

The truth is, everyone in this narrative—I mean, Joseph's father, brothers, and Joseph himself knew what the dream was about. They all had their interpretation of the dream. Everyone knew that Joseph was destined to be great, to be ruler, to lead, and to reign. The dream was discovered, uncovered, and now it had to be nurtured if it would see the light of the day.

By the way, Joseph's brothers and adversaries would stop at nothing to make him suffer. But Joseph's father only tried to talk Joseph out of his 'illusion.' Yet, Joseph would stop at nothing to see his dream come true. He kept the dreams in his heart. He became his own one-and-only fan, keeping the flame of hope in the storms of life.

Subsequently, Joseph was sold into slavery by his brothers because of his dreams. Life as a slave was a painful enigma. It felt like darkness compared to light. Joseph's life of ease, comfort, and care with Papa Jacob ended abruptly. Like a lily among thorns, Joseph chose to thrive and not just survive.

Stripped of his coat of many colours, he served under any condition as soon as he learned that leadership can be earned through service. Whereas he could have become bitter and sad at each of his life's phases, yet Joseph took courage and made the most of every moment. While in Potiphar's house, he served with so much diligence and integrity that Potiphar could completely place all he had in Joseph's care.

Potiphar's house became Joseph's fertile ground, and there he nurtured his dreams. He was able to develop his leadership skill, making himself ready and fit for the throne.

Now, there's an important point I want you to note here. The path to actualize Joseph's dream was never a usual ride, free from contradictions, variations, and distractions. So, no matter where you are in your journey, believe that you're not alone.

Potiphar's wife was another noisome disruption in Joseph's new normal at Potiphar's house. So, Potiphar's wife tried to seduce Joseph. But the man would not settle for less. His dream stiffened his spine; he refused to bend or bow.

You know, doesn't it feel perfect to be in charge? What more should a slave ask for? Potiphar's wife offered Joseph a position that felt like the best thing since sliced bread.

Though it looked like a dream come true, Joseph understood that Potiphar's wife was set to destroy his years of nurturing a dream. Even more, Joseph interpreted the temptation as a direct attack against his relationship with the giver of all pleasant dreams—God. Joseph refused to let that happen at whatever cost!

Did Joseph play with pest-Mrs-Potiphar? No! The bible records that, *"[Joseph] left his garment in her hand, and fled, and got him out."* - **Gen 39:12** Joseph's picture of his future became his light with which he navigated the dark and dangerous terrain of slavery and sin while in Potiphar's house.

Joseph's refusal to compromise brought him calculated attacks and severe punishments. Yet, it was all a blessing in disguise—a correct response to distractions to one's dream! Look at the outcome of joseph's refusal,

> *¹⁹ So it was, when his master heard the words which his wife spoke to him, saying, "Your servant did to me after this manner," that his anger was aroused.*
>
> *²⁰ Then Joseph's master took him and put him into the prison, a place where the king's prisoners were confined. And he was there in the prison.*
>
> **- Gen 39:19-20**

Even though Joseph was stripped of his clothes and position the second time and thrown into prison. Yet, Joseph was willing to keep serving with joy and happiness, even in prison. The reason was that he did not go into prison alone— he went with his dream! Therefore, he could not be broken by any challenge on his way to fulfilling his dream. Joseph remained resolute, positive, and focused!

> ²¹ But the Lord was with Joseph and showed him mercy, and He gave[a] him favour in the sight of the keeper of the prison.
>
> ²² And the keeper of the prison committed to Joseph's hand all the prisoners who were in the prison; whatever they did there, it was his doing.
>
> **- Gen 39:21-22**

While in prison, Joseph became a significant source of encouragement to the other prisoners—a king, yet without a crown. In fact, the keeper of the prison also committed everything into his care. Joseph understood that even the prison is an excellent place to nurture his dream and extent that one thing he had—interpreting of dreams, in blessing others. In the darkest moments of your life, you must learn to maintain a positive approach to life.

After a few years in prison, Joseph's moment to actualize his dream came, and he never missed that moment. And yes! Your moment will come, but will you be ready? Only the courageous-- those who have nurtured their dream would qualify for this kind of harvest—the transforming moment. There's that one moment that changes everything for the dreamer.

Certainly! People oppressed, abused, attacked, seduced, segregated, ostracised, and misjudged Joseph— the dreamer. Yet, Joseph kept his dreams alive by actively nurturing it for the big moment.

Eventually, Joseph's gift of dream interpretation brought him before the most powerful man in the world—Pharaoh, King of Egypt. Joseph's wisdom defied the most erudite astrologers. Even the king could not resist the shrewdness with which he solved the royal riddle. Despite spending many years in slavery and more in prison, Joseph never jettisoned his talent. Like a well-carved instrument, Joseph proved extremely valuable. He nurtured himself, his gifts, his character, and his dream to become the Hebrew born square peg in Egypt's square hole, fitting to lead and to save.

In no time, Joseph's story changed. All his pains and sacrifice paid off as rose to become the second in command to Pharaoh in Egypt. Interestingly, not only did his brothers bow to him, but Joseph also received obeisance from all the nations of the world in exchange for sustenance during a deadly 7-year famine.

Therefore, I challenge you to light up the fire of hope in your heart, no matter where you are right now. I challenge you to take up that one dream like a flaming sword and match forward to the next moments of your life, rest assured that your dreams would come true.

If Luther stood firm in the face of opposition and rejection— you could do the same! If Joseph had to show courage and conviction against challenges while actualizing his dream— you've got to be courageous!

William Faulkner once said, *"You cannot swim for new horizons until you dare to lose sight of the shore."* Yes! Your dream is accomplishable if you leap beyond your hurdles and stand against your opposition. Having a dream is great, but setting out with courage (nurturing your dream) is what makes for its actualization.

*ABUNDANCE OF ONE*

# CHAPTER
## *Seven*

### How To Bite And Breathe!

(The Place of Persistency and
Consistency in Fulfilling Your Vision)

> "It takes determination to see a dream come to pass. The question is not will you start, but will you finish."
>
> **- Joel Osteen**

Life does not hand anyone all they want; it only offers what we need. Hence, the need to learn how to maximize every opportunity even in the face of countless challenges. According to an article written by Rebecca Oconnell, "11 Solid

Facts About English Bulldog," "Bulldogs were bred to be a highly efficient bull-baiting machine. Their stocky bodies were good for keeping them grounded against a bull's best efforts to launch them into the air."

However, there's an interesting fact about bulldog's physiology that caught my attention. Rebecca highlighted that "Short snouts allowed them to breathe properly while firmly holding onto a bull's snout..." This is what I call the *bite-and-breathe tenacity*: a requisite for maximizing your life and fulfilling your mandate.

In life, we all need the bulldog's kind of bite-and-breathe tenacity. It is not just enough to take the bull by the horn, we must also strive hard to retain the horn and outlive the bull. Life is a race; without perseverance and determination to finish, challenges become barricades instead of propellants.

## DEREK REDMOND

Derek Redmond was an Olympic athlete whose life has a powerful lesson about what it means to bite and breathe. Even if you don't know that name, I bet you've heard the famous Olympic story of persistence and determination.

All through his brilliant career, Derek held the British record for the 400 meters sprint. He won Gold medals in the world championship and European championship.

But, at the Olympic Games held in Barcelona in 1992, Derek experienced the shock of his life. Suddenly, in the middle of one of the most notable games in his life—the most important sporting event in the world—Derek's hamstring tore. Running the 400 meters for Britain at the Olympic semi-final looked like a dream come true. But with this nasty sprain, Derek's dream was about to become a nightmare.

Naturally, people wouldn't mind if an athlete trips and falls. So, Derek had good reasons to fall off the track and cry "mayday"! He was young and determined, he could quit the semi-finals and try again after 4 years (the next Olympic Games).

On the contrary, Derek chose the tougher option. The option to keep on keeping on. Despite the pain and discomfort, Dereck continued limping right to the finish line—with the help of his father, who stepped up to support his *never-say-never* son.

Even though he had won many gold medals and awards, running for Britain, the Olympics medal could have been another dream come true. Nevertheless, Derek understood that running in the Olympics is a dream come true in itself, and he was committed to making it count.

The beautiful thing about Derek's story is not just the fact that he persevered to the end of that race, but the eternal fame and recognition that he earned by such a heroic act. On that fateful day, Derek earned a standing ovation from the crowd. Even though he was disqualified, nonetheless, his persistence and perseverance were never forgotten.

Today, only a few remember the winner of that particular semi-final (and many more semi-finals before and after that). But Derek is fondly remembered by many till this very day. This incidence became a well-remembered moment in Olympic history, and it's also used in advertisements by Visa to represent the Olympic spirit.

So, what does it mean to bite and breathe? It is the bull-dog persistence that drives any vision until it becomes a reality, notwithstanding the level of opposition that you encounter in life.

While running with your vision, consistency, and persistence are twin essentials for guaranteed success. Remember that, if you don't value your dream, sacrificing to see it manifest will feel like a luxury-- an unnecessary extra and vain exertion. I have discovered that there is no star in any field of human endeavour without their scars! Failure is not an end in itself, but a script that can be re-written if you engage the twin essentials of persistence and consistency.

## THOMAS EDISON

Thomas Edison conducted 1000 failed experiments, and the 1001st was the light bulb. What do you think? 1000 times! And he persisted consistently on getting his desired end—his vision! Can you believe that? Indeed, you've not failed until you fail to persevere. Think about Reggie Jackson. He struck out 2600 times in his career. That is the most in the history of baseball, but you don't hear about the strikeouts. People only remember the home runs. You must understand that every failed experiment is one closer step to success.

Take risk! Never quit or retrieve! You may have the talent and skill to succeed, but the question is, do you have guts to fail? Sometimes, failure is the best way to know where you're going is worth all it takes! Dan Gable, an Olympic Wrestling medallist, once said, *"Gold medals aren't really made of Gold. They're made of sweat, determination, and a hard-to-find alloy called guts."*

On your journey to success, encountering setbacks is inevitable, but you must not end your success story in defeat. The inability to persist is a sure indication of failure, don't give in.

Many shrivel up when they encounter difficulties in the pursuit of their vision. At the sight of little opposition, negativity, and trouble, they are willing to throw in the towel. But the best success stories are based on failures that turned into phenomenal achievements. In truth, what cripples so many destinies are a lack of faith, rising out of fear! Fear of failure, fear of the unknown, or even the fear of success. However, what gives persistence in the pursuit of your vision is faith, faith in the process. This is the antidote for fear.

## FACE YOUR FEARS

> *"He who is not every day conquering some fear has not learned the secret of life."*
> **- Ralph Waldo**

Bravery is never the absence of fears but the ability to conquer them! Indeed, in fulfilling your vision, you may be confronted with situations like Gordian knots to untie. However, coming face to face with your fears, how you handle them will determine your course in life. Each of us, at some points in our lives, must confront our fears. Failure to confront your fears with inner strength will only limit the fulfilment of your vision. John Maxwell said, *"The only guarantee for failure is to stop trying."*

I must say at this point that indecision is the fuel of fear and doubt. But when you're set to face your fear and take a deliberate step in reaching your goal, your confidence, and courage increases. Do you know what happens when you result to fear? Your path to success suddenly becomes darkened and twisted. You develop unnecessary mental and emotional clutter! Therefore, never be afraid to fail or think outside the box.

## NOW, HOW DO YOU FACE YOUR FEAR?

- Be definite about your purpose, desire, and passion. A profound statement Jesus made that underscores definiteness of purpose is recorded in John 9:4, *"I **must** work the works of him that sent me, **while it is day: the night cometh**, when no man can work."* Your sense of purpose must be salted with passion and sincere desire to fulfill it in due time! We must be deliberately conscious of TIME!

➢ Be definite about your plans— Dreams without the correct setting and actualization of goals are just nightmares. Obstacles become apparent when your gaze shifts from your goal. Stay focused!

➢ Get accurate knowledge— Journeying into your vision should never be by assumption. It is important to note what you know and what you don't know. It's not a thing of shame to admit you don't know something, not seeking knowledge is what cripples even the greatest of visions. Also, you must convert your knowledge into the correct application of life—which is wisdom.

➢ Develop a strong network— Having people of like-mind around you provides the right support system: mentors, teachers, expert advisers, and more. People who can help chart your way through the storms with their wealth of experience.

➢ Check your habits—Persistence is the direct result of habit. Restructure your daily routine, check the content of your character, and tie up every loose end!

## CHOOSING FAITH OVER FEAR

> *"For whatsoever is **born of God** overcomes **the world**: and this is **the victory that** overcomes the world, **even our faith**."*
>
> **- 1 John 5:4**

We said earlier that faith is an antidote for fear. But now, let's look more deeply into that. The first guarantee for overcoming fear using the lens of John is that you are born of God! There is an inner capacity in everyone who is born of God has to conquer every fear—it is called faith!

Imagine yourself in a difficult situation with no hope of escape. But then, you hear the voice of your father resounding from Deuteronomy 3:18 behind you saying, *"I will never leave you nor forsake you. Do not be afraid; do not be discouraged."*— How will you feel?

Finally, think about this verse of scripture; *"Perfect love casts out fear"*—1John 4:18. What do you discover? Perfect love! When you walk in love, fears find its way out of your mind. Your love for what you are called to do empowers you to laugh in the face of danger and thumb your nose at risk.

For instance, imagine your little boy or girl walking down the path of a moving train. Horrific, right? But I'm sure you will defy all odds to save your kid. Even though getting your kid out of such a perilous situation is risky, you'll be willing to do it. Why? Because your love for your kid has conquered the fear of the approaching train.

The same applies to your vision and dream; if you're passionate about your dream, all odds will only be a stepping stone to your victory. Moreover, I have often discovered that the fascinating part of anyone's success story is how they failed. So, move courageously through your night into the brightness of your morning.

## THE WISDOM OF PATIENCE

> *"For **the vision** is yet for **an appointed time**, but at **the end**, it shall speak, and not lie: **though it tarry, wait for it; because it will surely come, it will not tarry.**"*
>
> **- Habakkuk 2:3**

In the face of growing technology and innovation in the world today, things we do with much energy are now done faster and easier. As good as these things are, it's capable of making us unsettled and impatient. I mean, our sense of waiting can quietly be undermined, and you begin to think delay means denial.

The word patience simply means enduring and waiting in the face of suffering. But not everyone who waits for God waits with patience. Think about the verse above. The vision is yet for *an appointed* time! For every vision, there is divine timing. Your understanding that there is a factor (Timing) in the actualization of your vision makes you rest and prepare adequately for it. Listen to this: No vision speaks at the beginning! Every vision looks weak and improbable at the beginning. But in the end, it shall **speak.**

Everything that comes as a challenge to you in the pursuit of your vision is but a light affliction. And you know what? It works in you a deep and far exceeding and eternal glory. Those challenges are not meant to crush you but strengthen you! Look at what Paul unveiled in 2 Corinthians 4:17- "For our **light affliction,** which is but **for a moment,** worketh for us a far more exceeding and eternal **weight of glory;**"

The journey into your vision must be engaged with a high level of patience and endurance. "*Wherefore seeing we also are* *compassed about with so great a cloud of witnesses, let us lay aside every weight, and the sin which doth so easily beset us, and let **us run with patience the race that is set before us**, Looking unto Jesus the author and finisher of our faith; who **for the joy** that **was set before him** endured the cross, despising the shame, and is set down **at the right hand of the throne of God**."* **Hebrew 12:1-2**

When a player handles the ball on a pitch, what he thinks about is not just the ball but the goal post. He keeps enduring every attack just to score a goal. Therefore, when the Bible motivates you to run, it's with a target in mind. That's the point! You must pursue your vision with the end in view.

Why was Jesus able to sustain the capacity to endure something as unfriendly as the cross? ***"The joy that was set before Him!"*** His gaze was not set on present and momentary pain His vision brings, but at the end of His vision! That was the reason He could endure the down moments of his call or vision.

Finally, there is blessing perseverance brings to your life. Look at James 1:12," *Blessed is the man that **endureth temptation**: for when **he is tried**, he shall receive **the crown of life**, which the Lord hath promised to them that love him.*" When you're able to endure the temptation of stepping out of your vision and throwing in the towel, you're given the crown of life. You should acknowledge that no success trophy is lifted without consistency and persistence. *The abundance of one* is only sustained in the lives of men who understand the place of endurance and patience. Remain strong!

# CHAPTER

## *Eight*

### Leveraging Divine Advantage

> "But **the people** that do **know their God** shall be **strong**, and **do exploits**."
> **- Daniel 11:32**

The determination to harness and maximize the potentials and resources available to you is a prerequisite for success in life. Every human being has a gift or skill that affords them some advantage. But the question is, do we know how to maximize what we've got, whether good or bad? This is what leverage means – maximizing potential.

Life is like a football match, everybody is competing to reach a goal, and most people are willing to succeed at the expense of others. In this highly competitive reality, one has to have something extra to survive and thrive.

Do you know that life is all about leverage? Consider the air we breathe. We maximize it daily to stay alive. What about the times and seasons? We use them to grow our crops, number our days, and much more.

Also, think about inventions and technological innovations - products of leveraging the power and creativity of the mind. Ever since electricity was discovered, humanity has been leveraging its limitless possibilities to improve our standard of living.

In the same vein, God also wants His children to leverage their relationship with him in their daily lives. The scripture above reveals that having intimacy with God makes you extraordinarily strong and a producer of tremendous results. What this means is, knowing God gives you an advantage beyond the physical realm. It gives you a divine advantage.

Moreover, it makes you walk in a realm of no limits and exploit. Your relationship with God provides you a platform, an edge over the Average Joe - he is not in connection with God. Your intimacy with God should afford you strength beyond the ordinary in the pursuit of your assignment.

Prof. Ian I. Mitroff, a business professor, while researching companies for his book *"A spiritual audit of corporate America,"* discovered that "*Spirituality could be the ultimate competitive advantage."* This is actually in agreement with the biblical perspective on the advantage of leveraging your intimacy with God.

Look at what God said in Jeremiah 32:27 as an assurance to those who know Him: *"Behold, I am* **the LORD,** *the God of all flesh: is there anything too hard for me?"* God wants you to maximize His Ability. Indeed, divine advantage takes you above the limitations of man into the possibilities of God.

Think about the profound question God asked in the scripture above. Make a list of all that seems like unsurmountable mountain and place that question before it—is it difficult for God to do? Your divine advantage grants you an unerring ability to foresee challenges before it comes. It gives you the capacity to bring to light, witty inventions, and strength to stand in times of challenges.

Let's take a look at examples of people who leveraged on divine advantage and the results it birthed in their lives.

## INTIMACY AND FORESIGHT

Knowing the future through intimacy with God was a recurrent experience of Daniel. Daniel was a political leader in Babylon, who, through his ability to leverage on his divine advantage, secured a significant voice in Babylon—a foreign land. He was in a foreign land, but he was able to influence the policies of the land by simply leveraging on the divine advantage he had. In Daniel two, we read of Nebuchadnezzar's dream. He had a dream but soon forgot the dream. Nebuchadnezzar then summoned all the magicians, enchanters, sorcerers, and magicians to tell him his dream and its interpretation. These magicians, enchanters, sorcerers, and magicians could not bring an answer to the king. Amid such a confusing and trying moment, Daniel and his friends leveraged on divine advantage in knowing the king's dream and gained foresight into its interpretation.

*"Then Daniel went in and desired of the king that he would give him time and that he would shew the king **the interpretation.** Then Daniel went to his house and made the thing known to Hananiah, Mishael, and Azariah, his companions: **That they would desire mercies of the God of heaven concerning this secret;** that Daniel and his fellows*

*should not perish with the rest of the wise men of Babylon. Then was **the secret revealed** unto Daniel in a night vision. Then Daniel blessed the God of heaven."*

Daniel and his friends understood the advantage they had above all the astrologers and magicians. So, they engaged it and got an insight into the dream of Nebuchadnezzar and foresight into what the dream will bring upon the king.

Imagine what Daniel said, *"that Daniel and his fellows should not perish with the rest of the wise men in Babylon."* You see, you must know that what you have is capable of giving you an edge over a nation. The secret was revealed to him, and he was able to save himself and his friends. This divine advantage keeps you from casualties and unnecessary losses.

In the stock market today, predictions are essential to how successful investors make their investments. However, research has shown that there are reasons why these predictions may not work. I mean, even the Federal Reserve Chairman gets it wrong. But you know, many who have this advantage aren't aware they can use it in the stock market to get tremendous results and save their economy.

Think about it: how many investments have you made and lost much money? How many business proposals have you written that failed? What if you had allowed God to properly guide all your decision? How successful would you be?

Think about Joseph, how he accurately predicted the famine that was to happen seven-years. He literally saved the economy of Egypt from crumbling because he knew how to leverage divine advantage.

## BOUNCING BACK AFTER SUFFERING GREAT LOSS

In first Samuel 30, David and his soldiers had just returned to Ziklag to find their city destroyed and burnt down. The Amalekites perpetrated the wreckage. They plundered the city and took their wives, daughter, and sons as captives.

David's loss was so much that even though he had lost his family, his soldiers—his partners—thought of stoning him. Why? They believed it was his fault. Now, when everyone you expect to bring you encouragement in life turn against you, what do you do? When your followers no longer trust your leadership, what do you do? When all you have laboured for goes down the drain with no hope of recovery, what do you do?

After David wept thoroughly, notice what he did in bringing back all that he had lost. *"And David was greatly distressed; for the people spake of stoning him, because the soul of all the people was grieved, every man for his sons and for his daughters:* **but David encouraged himself in the LORD his God."** Indeed, there will come times in our lives when all around us standstill, and nothing seem to be working. In those times, what do we do? Upgrade! Connect to your divine advantage. Then, what conquers and overcomes others will be your stepping stone.

You know, nobody was there to encourage David, but he encouraged himself in the Lord. He connected to a realm of inexhaustible help. Aren't you surprised at his actions? The natural thing would have been to mark outright strategies for recovery. Instead, he leveraged on the divine advantage. In truth, you will struggle less if you can only tap into your divine resources.

## DAVID'S INQUIRY

> ⁷ And David said to Abiathar the priest, the son of Ahimelech, "Bring me the ephod." So Abiathar brought the ephod to David.
>
> ⁸ And David inquired of the Lord, "Shall I pursue after this band? Shall I overtake them?" He answered him, "Pursue, for you shall surely overtake and shall surely rescue.
>
> **- 1 Samuel 30:7-8**
> (English Standard Version)

What was David's inquiry? Where did he inquire from? Well, David asked whether or not he should pursue the band of riders, and he inquired from God. Why? David had an understanding that the only final guarantee for his victory is his divine advantage. I mean, no one was even there to encourage or assure him—save God.

When last, did you effectively engage your divine advantage before making any business decision?

When last did you inquire from God concerning a vital life decision? You need the all-knowing God to have a secured battle plan.

Did David recover all? Yes! David recovered all, and he bounced back from impoverishment to abundance.

Take a look at the outcome of David's inquiry, *"And David recovered all that the Amalekites had carried away: and David rescued his two wives.* **And there was nothing lacking to them,** *neither small nor great, neither sons nor daughters, neither spoil nor anything that they had taken to them:* **David recovered all***."* 1 Samuel 30: 18-19.

Finally, all of life's successes are the results of leverage. And as children of God, our heavenly father wants us to make use of everything he has made available to reign in life. He desires that our results and achievements are beyond this natural realm. God has called us to show forth His praises by tapping into His unending resources. Failure, limitations, and the impossibilities associated with human life should be a thing of the past. And this can only happen when you leverage on divine advantage.

Remember, in you is The Abundance of One.

*God Bless You!*

Printed in Great Britain
by Amazon